Turn to Salt

Poems & Lyrics

Teresa Staley

2017

Turn to Salt
Teresa Staley

Copyright ® 2017 Teresa Staley

ISBN: 9781974036783
First Edition

All rights reserved. No portion of this book may be reproduced in any form without permission from the author, except for brief excerpts for reviews and criticism.

"Moss Bank Crafts" and "Andrew As a Seagull" first appeared in Blue Pitcher.

Cover Design by Ruthie Katzenstein
Cover Art: "The Wolf You Feed Will Win the Fight" Noah Howard
Back cover photo: "Teresa in the Rain" Dick Howard
Tattoo art: Matt Shelton, Paula Enscore

To my mom, Doris, who first spotted the spark.

And to all my friends and family along the way who fanned the flames.

Introduction

"Mid-life Offensive" was the original title of this book, not just because it is the first poem in this volume, but because for years folks I know have been after me to write my memoirs. I figured if I collected my poetry -- if I used an offensive tactic -- I could push that project back a bit until I was ready to bare myself to the world. It never occurred to me that if memoirs are the body search in security, poetry is the x-ray.

The title shifted to "Splay" (too sexually suggestive), then to "Volatility" (too aggressive.) I landed on Turn to Salt. I recognize the pitfalls of the allusion to the story of Lot's wife, but I wanted to use a line from one of the poems. And I wanted to bring home the idea that backwards reflection may not be the spiritually fulfilling experience it's cracked up to be. It might be downright painful. Then again, as one friend pointed out, salt is essential to maintain life.

I began exploring the writing of poetry at age 12. I was intrigued by how words could distill and preserve an experience. I continued to study the art under the tutelage of such masters as Ron Bayes while I attended St. Andrews Presbyterian College (now University.) I learned from him how to compress experience into the most meaningful space.

From Bob Watson, professor in the MFA Writing program at UNCG, I adopted the mantra, "Be honest. Be kind." From Lee Zacharias in the same program, I learned the craft of storytelling. And from Fred Chappell, my chief thesis advisor. I discovered how my writing mirrored the patterns of my life. During our final critique of my thesis before its submission, he turned to me and said, "Darlin', you keep meeting the same guy over and over, don't you?" Indeed.

So, in these pages, you will find poems of love and longing and contemplation. To those of you who recognize yourselves, take it personally. It means you made an impression in my life. Good or bad, you changed me. I believe all interactions happen for a reason. No regrets.

To those of you who are reading these poems and lyrics for the first time, thank you. A few of the pieces I feel would be enhanced by brief explanations: "Sinkhole" and "Bridge" are companion pieces. They are meant to be read together as the Summer of 2007 Disaster Poems. My father literally helped build the road in Greensboro that sank. The bridge that collapsed was in Minnesota and I was struck by how the casualties were identified by divers reading license plates by touch in the murky water. "Poem for Mattie" refers to Mattie Stepanek, a fellow poet with muscular dystrophy who died in the summer of 2004. I hope you find something in these lines that resonates with you.

In recent years, I moved from writing poetry to songwriting. (An early attempt at writing country songs when I was 14 thankfully did not see the light.) Influenced at first by Matt Bostick and Scott Pryor, then by Bart Trotman and Noah Howard as my skills developed, I have written songs with numerous friends, including Emily Zeanah Shelton and Emily Stewart. I find this experience more enriching than writing poetry, and I plan to continue down this path. Collaboration is much less lonely. Thanks to those who share creative space with me.

Finally, I would like to thank Erin Hayes, Jerrod Smith, Dick Howard, and Ruthie Katzenstein for their contributions in the development of this book. And a special thanks to Jon Obermeyer, who reminded me that time is not a guarantee in life and threw down the gauntlet to finish this project before my 60th birthday. It is done.

Turn to Salt

CONTENTS
Poems

Mid-life Offensive	5
Artemisia	6
Splay	7
The Papermaker	8
Picture: The Reunion of Two College Friends	9
Moss Bank Crafts	10
Volatility	11
Labels	12
Hospital	13
Mute	14
Andrew As a Seagull	15
Lines	16
Figure It Out	17
Growing Pains	18
Map	19
Three Fingers, You Drown	22
The Weight of Your Arm Is a Solid Thing	23
Birdbath	24
Wind-Up	25
Portrait of Reticence	26
Diviner	27
Collector's Items	28
Nebraska Mourning	29
Sinkhole	30
Bridge	31
Night Noises	32
Term of Endearment	33
Poem for Mattie	34
The Conversation	35
Station	36
A Dozen Things You Taught Me	37
Act Four, Scene One	38
Age	39
At the Rest, Home	40
On the Death of Harold the Cat	41

Lyrics
Things Unrecorded							42
So...									44
Diminishing								46
Gardener and the Pruner						47
<3 vs. $								48

About the Author							50

"I love you — and yet — and yet — I love you."

- Randall Jarrell, *A Girl in a Library*

Mid-Life Offensive

The small tufts of down
above your knuckles
salute your youth,
serve as a lookout for
territories conquered:
been there, fought the battles,
moved on

but the belly-creep of
invisible velvet
on your inner wrists
underneath my fingertips
scales the fortress,
captures the sentry,
invades my war-weary heart.

Artemisia

The gift arrives two weeks after Christmas:
    a pair of graying handkerchiefs
      clumsily stitched into a sachet,
      mismatched threads
          (what was on the bobbin and
            whatever else was handy),
    askew square encasing
    a stale tobacco, cork-scented herb.
It is artemisia,
the moon to hunt dreams by,
a thoughtful present,
the past held captive to spring forth from pillows.
It is wormwood,
    absinthe,
        this absence from you.

Splay

I want to splay my soul
for you, fall like a
baby bird with undeveloped feet
from branches spread wide
defy gravity, fly.
Look at me dance
from this slanted doorway,
ungainly pigeon-toed girl.
Whirl around,
watch me again
through this beveled window,
red-haired woman
with the private grin.

The Papermaker - from Folk Arts City Stage 1984

I find a spot at the demonstration table.
"You place your hand
deep in the vat and stir
until the fibers
are evenly dispersed."
He pours the blue-gray potion
onto a screen
turned onto a blotter.
After the show,
we examine his broadsides:
poems printed on shredded
stems and petals of dandelions.
I want my words bleeding
into his fibers.

Picture: The Reunion of Two College Friends

Abracadabra, they pose before velvet.
Gloveless, he reaches into his back pocket,
pulls long balloons out, and fashions bright animals --
cobras and parrots and an elk with no hind legs.
      They call it a mermoose,
            their small, private joke.
Presto! Change-o! She calls for the blade --
metal obstruction to hold them apart.
She fears for her past: is he less than remembered?
He slices her stomach instead of her heart.
Jerked like a rabbit from a tall silk hat,
Witness Illusion where Magic once sat.

Moss Bank Crafts

Shards of Indian pottery
uncovered by a young entrepreneur
captured in woven leather pendants
the loose ends braided into a necklace.
Dig me up from this earth, please,
for I am old and brittle
and will break at your touch,
gladly.

Volatility

Toasting,
I raise my glance.
Your intensity scorches across crowds,
    the seas part
  and there you stand,
      sure enough,
fresh from some invisible storm.
Now, here you sit.
I know nothing and everything about you,
    study your eyes for familiar ground,
        find Mauna Loa, Kilauea resting.
My foothold slips as you shift in your seat,
    elbows on knees, head turned sideways
        to take me in.
In the midst of conversation,
    I circle, pacing,
  testing, searching for strongholds.
My fingers ache as I grip
    the precipice;
Your fingers lock behind your neck
    as you lean back,
  simmering composure.
Your laughter ripples like lava:
    Hoi hoi. Aa.
And I slide into the crater, smiling.

Labels

I wear my label inside of my underwear
    hidden in the back,
        where no one can see it,
            not even me.
Society wrote it in on the day I was born,
    with washable ink
    that fades with hope
        and reappears with pain.
You wear your label on the front of your shirt
  an alligator, hand-stitched in bitterness
(or maybe it's a crocodile,
but don't
    try to fool me:
I know the tears are real.)
    Your label is etched with indelible ink
        that never washes out,
            even when you want it to --
                be careful.

Hospital

On the brink,
    I saw lizards;
    I heard grandmother's silence;
    I knew seamless darkness;
    I felt other hands trembling
        in mine.

Returning,
    I felt hunger;
    I knew mystery;
    I heard music hissing;
    I saw blood, mine,
                red.

Rejoicing,
    I saw

Mute

Sometimes at night
I'm glad I'm mute
when the nurse pushes
the syringe
that inflates the cuff
on the end of my trach,
seals my voice
behind the breaths
the ventilator
sends into me.
The nurse listens
but doesn't note
the gasp as I fall
off a cliff again:
the "oohs" and "aahs"
as I soar without wings,
the screams as a tiger
paws at my skin.
Most of the time
I'm glad I'm mute at night,
especially when I
whisper your name --
as if you could
hear me anyway
five hundred miles,
twenty years,
a marriage away.

Andrew as a Seagull

He runs,
    flails arms in the rhythmic
    flutter of wings,
    feathers hidden under tousled hair,
    baseball shirt,
    faded jeans.
        Child of my neighbor,
        strange kin,
        born on the day of my operation,
        you should have been delivered
        to me.
His call's so real,
the autumn breeze turns to salt.

Lines

See this line,
the one here? --
    It's yours.
It adds character to my eyes,
       don't you think?
I know
    it adds desperation
to my style...

Figure It Out

My heart
encrypted, a code:
break me.

Growing Pains

We grow.
We grow smart.
We grow rebellious.
We grow wild.
We "grow up."
We grow silent.
We grow bold.
We grow friendly.
We grow cold.
We grow wiser.
We grow together.
We grow older.
We grow careless.
We grow apart.
We grow lonely.
We grow cynical.
We grow
      plants.

Map

No one knows we are here.
We rise in glass through concrete
to this space.
This vista overlooks
the sluggish traffic pulse of Greensboro;
Koury and the University;
Towers and heat lightning
flash in the distance.

We have come to read each other
poetry. But first you spin
my attention to the sky,
try to capture the image
with your camera, sigh
that this almost never works.
The clouds layer purple
over the night blue.
Venus appears to be
spit from the moon.
Words fail me, too.

A lone red Ford Taurus
circles the lot. A couple
waves, pulls into a spot
within view. You give
me that look that illuminates
the world. That grin.
As we settle in, awareness of their
presence slips away.

You begin with a poem
defending iceberg lettuce;
my first lauds the
value of writing letters.

And so we continue
for over two hours,
explain our choices.
No one hears our voices
pushed away by the breeze,
the way you brush my hair
from my face.

The pop of the cork
on our bottle of wine
fades. Even our image
on your digital screen
falls away to the corners
of the frame.
No ghosts of old lovers stay.
They approach and vanish
as if they respect this holy moment.

No one knows
we are in this place.
You end with Seamus Heaney
digging earth. I finish
with Randall Jarrell
longing in a library:
so many words to
excavate one line.

The couple emerges
from the deck below,
acknowledges a good-bye,
drives away.
They were never here.
No map defines this terrain.
Nothing marks this page
as you pack to go,
save for your christening
of our chosen pavement
with the last of the Shiraz,

we and God our only witness
to this hello.

Three Fingers -- You Drown

Before the wave;
Before the bubbles bursting
    on the surface;
Before the cries for help
and the murmur of names;
Before the tears meld with the sea;
Before the struggle and the reaching;
Before the death gasp;
Before the calm;
Before three fingers,
    sinking,
I will turn my back on the grisly scene,
Believing we could have made it.

The Weight of Your Arm Is a Solid Thing

The weight of your arm is a solid thing
Across my stomach, your hand in mine:
Proof of your presence beyond my dreams.

The slope of your face lulls my heart to sing;
Your even breathing frames this time.
The weight of your arm is a solid thing.

Light drifts through windows in flickering streams,
This Sunday morning bed our shrine,
Proof of your presence beyond my dreams.

Perhaps in the future this memory will sting
As we search for some meaning that won't be defined.
The weight of your arm is a solid thing.

I relish this loneliness parting brings,
Search linens for hair: none match your kind,
Proof of your presence beyond my dreams.

Without love, absence is abstract it seems:
The physical alters, becomes the divine.
The weight of your arm is a solid thing.
Proof of your presence beyond my dreams.

Birdbath

   My throat grows tired
      from singing myself;
To bathe in your waters
     would be so lovely
  only, you are as still as ice,
and though I screech and flutter,
    my reflection
draws no nearer
   to your surface.

Wind-up

Give me time
   to reckon
  with reality
    again.
Smile in place:
   There
      check
makeup intact
      check
Now push me back
   into the world
    and watch me go --
    simple as one,
      two,
  fro.

Portrait of Reticence

She has the advantage
of her youth
as vast as a field of clover
which she mails
in four-leaf packages
to her would-be lover.
She has the luxury
of giving luck away,
this Amelia
of the lithe body
and adoring glances
who chooses friendship
over taking chances.

I am the cinema's Amelie
but clothed in older skin
holding love at arm's length,
not wanting to give in.
I haunt the subways
of Paris, post messages
travel in disguise
while hoping he spies
the true nature of my heart
that beats stronger
in his presence
yet struggles
to keep us apart.

Diviner

On the top of your head,
I can read your future:
small white creek under black
destined to become a lake.
If I could find a way,
I would take my hand,
wave it over the terrain
of your skin, freeze you
in your beautiful summer
before the pain of winter sets in.

Collector's Items

1. You don't have to bitch at me again.
   I know you stub your toes
   on the boxes of comics under the bed.
   I will move them.   I promise.

2. Besides, I need a spot for my hope chest
   of napkins from the weddings of friends;
   mint cups from baby showers;
   eighteen years of personal letters;
   paper umbrellas from Hawaiian luaus;
   some grade reports; old flight information;
   my autographed photo of Scott Hamilton,
   hands grabbing toes as he skates off a mountain.

3. "One match," you say, "our goose is cooked."

4. Just you wait. One day,
   I will be discovered;
   "She is rich, you know,
   because - -"
   (the story will go)
   "- - she held on to what other folks overlook."

Nebraska Mourning

I didn't know you then,
holder of broken ballerinas.
"The focus wasn't on..."
You slip, offstage,
    your humanness throwing you
    to your knees:
in smoke-laced San Francisco delicatessens,
over Kona sunsets,
these thoughts,
    these moods, move me,
and on second glance,
we have never been strangers,
    we only met late.

Sinkhole

We travelled with abandon
over the smooth gray face
until the great eye opened
and I fell into space
paralyzed by the sight
of the distance
from severed connections to land.
Water roars,
raises me to understand:
my father poured the pavement,
my mother laid the pipes.

Bridge

1.
The plunge wasn't sought
like a thrill dive off a high cliff
but a falling away
of terra firma,
an abrupt shift in the rote journey
from here to there.

2.
My fingers grope the cold unfamiliar,
search the murkiness
for numbers remembered,
struggle to make sense of
the spaces between letters,
one submersion bubbling clearer:
I do not want to wave goodbye
to the face I found in the rear view mirror.

Night Noises

God must have been distracted
while designing the hermit crab
says shell expert Elva Sheets.
If so His chief assistant
must have been tapped
to complete the order of
my pairs of ears:
a mother's ears in a
single body.

I hear
my own mother's
nightmare scream
as she turns,
faces passing time;
my father's cough
the gurgle of cigarette suicide:
the rhythm of
your breath
in faraway beds
not mine.

Term of Endearment

Word slips,
drips
from your mouth
to my ears,
honey
spilled in the gears of our relations,
stickies conversation,
jams up the tone,
sweetens the fear
that accidents happen.
That they don't.

Poem for Mattie

On the day you left us
for a better world,
I wasn't aware.
At the beach at the time,
I was learning to run
not to or from
but for the sheer joy
of movement through dark salt
air, the stars a roadmap
to nowhere.

Around us, all evaporates:
conversation; relationships;
lines drawn in the sand,
your hands on my wheelchair,
your feet in flip flops
slapping the bridge.

We are one body
pushing through the night
without thought or gender,
past or future:
spirit in flight.

The Conversation

In this Barbara Walters conversation
turned upside down,
you tell me
what animal I am:

blesbok,
a small antelope
indigenous to
South Africa,
Damaliscus dorcas phillipsi.
Diurnal feeders
on grass born after brushfire,
seekers of shade.
They cannot jump,
but crawl under obstacles.
The females protect their young,
threaten other females
but will not lock horns.
She lives her life
behind a kabuki mask,
her face a long white blaze,
thin brown lines down the sides
like tear tracks.

From dappled skin
through sweet giraffe eyes,
you watch her run,
elegant and free.

Station

This is meant to be a temporary stop
On the way home to more familiar faces,
So why am I tempted to linger here
To study the lines and destinations?

The whistle calls me to other warmth --
Arms circle me in close embraces.
Reluctantly, I board this train
That carries me to such distant places.

I find my way to the farthest point,
Toss flowers along the receding track:
I want to remember where I was
In case I should want to travel back.

I do what's safe; I compromise --
I leave the way station of your eyes.

A Dozen Things You Taught Me

An infant tugging on your hair
makes it grow stronger.
An adult manipulating your desire
makes you grow weaker.
A bee sting carefully positioned
eases physical pain.
A sarcastic barb deftly spoken
causes psychic distress.
A roof can only be shingled twice.
A shelter can be destroyed into infinity.
Certain blood types should avoid particular foods.
Certain heart types should avoid ingesting cynicism.
When the cold sets in,
you have twenty minutes
until the rain falls.
When the mood sets in,
you have no time before
the tears come.
If your hair blows into
your eyes,
turn and face the direction
of the wind.
If your mocking eyes
gaze into mine again,
Run.

Act Four, Scene One

There
on the table
the guest register.
There
the doors
the audience passes through.
There
on the wall
wreaths of flowers
with shocking red ribbons.
There is
the director
a red-haired praying mantis of a man
with bulging, bloodshot eyes.
There is
his assistant
fumbling after the crank in his
pocket.
There is the corpse --
they are cranking it closed now.
There is a woman
beside me, softly breathing garlic --
I am grateful.
It kills the sterile stench.
Who wrote this script?
I want to see the playwright:
It is my right.
There is
organ music that wafts and wafts.
There is funeral silence.

Age

I see my parents
shrink beneath their skin.
As old dreams burst,
the wrinkles set in;
as pace and sight falter,
an absence of grin --

I race to the mirror
to watch Age begin.

At the Rest, Home

Before double doors,
on the end table
in the lobby
rests a magazine:
Departures.
Its glossy cover story
declares
"Your Own Private Italy"
While around the corner
rumbles murmurs
indecipherable lava
pools into words,
bubbles from
a white-haired woman:
Help me.
I'm alone.
Help me.
At my back,
a tap at first,
from the hand of a man
in rumpled clothes
then a push
from his chair
as he passes,
persistent,
into my path.
One small victory
until he forgets
where he goes.
Protected by my yellow slicker,
I break for home
through glass into
November rain,
two thin layers
to divide myself from Rome.

On the Death of Harold the Cat

Less than a minute ago,
    he gave a yawn to the world,
    the sunlight a halo surrounding his seated form,
    perched like a hood ornament on the neighbors' Ranger.
Just last week,
    he slept curled on the stump in our front yard.
    I had never considered photography before I met him,
    this one-eared shadow
    slipping like gold sand through our red azaleas.
Now he is gone
    to the teeth of a car
    one thin stream to mark his passing
    the way I trickle ink on pages
    an attempt to preserve in words
    those things in life I cannot save.

Things Unrecorded

The money I spent
to show that I care:
look in my checkbook --
The numbers aren't there.
The pain that you cost me
Will not be rewarded:
these things go unrecorded.

Look in my journal --
The pages are white.
The memories of our time
Will not see the light.
I won't write the history
Of love that's aborted:
Some things go unrecorded.

So, I won't sing this song,
Won't hear the beat
Won't feel the pressure
When you turn up the heat.
I'm not your string puppet --
I'm cutting the ties.
If I won't admit our first hello,
Won't have to say goodbye.

The nights we drank too much wine,
Nights that we fought,
Nights I couldn't find my way
Out of thought.
I can't read this map,
My perception's
distorted:
Some paths go unrecorded.

So I won't record this song,
Won't feel the beat
Won't fall to pressure
When you turn up the heat.
I'm not your string puppet
I'm cutting the ties.
If I don't admit our first hello,
I won't have to say goodbye
Won't say goodbye.

So...

Can't see the features
of your silhouette
Backlit by fluorescence
from the day care
As you stand in the parking lot, I'm ready to go.
But beneath a slight fingernail moon
that softens the black of the sky
I can't see your voice,
read the mood in your eyes
As you say our new phase
Is defined by this phrase: so...

So, your Jameson whiskey
sends chills down my throat,
burns down the words
I choked on last night --
I know that you're right, but
it's so hard to swallow
the can'ts that dance between us.

So, it's another 3:30 rhyme:
our time together
is so cherished now
that sleeping seems so
superficial somehow.
So, our story has yet to unfold,
the ending so far in the future.
At least that's the hope
as you're packing to go.

So, your Jameson whiskey
sent chills down my throat,
burnt out the words that
I choked on that night;
I fight tears, but it's so

hard to swallow
the fears we can't name between us,
the can'ts that dance between us.

Diminishing
I heard I was a silent baby,
I know I was a quiet child,
Until I found my voice,
Want to make the crowds go wild,
Increase my noise
So I don't understand
The peace you've found
Without making a sound,
I just don't get why
You want to be diminishing,
Sliding through the cracks,
Not looking back,
Find yourself diminishing,
No flash or spark,
Don't disturb the dark.
I heard you missed Willie Nelson
When he came to Batteries Plus.
You were busy talking to Jesus
As he carried the cross
Down Battleground Road
Gathering crowd,
He turned to you and he asked out loud,
He said, "Hey man, are you going our way?"
You said, "No, I'm going to lunch today.
My body needs replenishing."
I want to spread my vision,
You want to stay the course.
You want to speak in whispers,
I'll sing until I'm hoarse,
Until I make my point,
I heard you anyway.
Before you start diminishing,
Sliding through the cracks,
Not looking back,
Find yourself diminishing,
All fades to black.
Find yourself diminishing.

Gardener and The Pruner (Teresa Staley and Noah Howard)

It's in the nature of the dove
To fly as far as it can go:
Magician wants to clip its wings
To get it ready
For the evening show.

Tiger pacing back-and-forth
Behind the bars that make a cage
Manufactured by which of us:
Which of us is on display?

Is the cowboy duty bound
To stoke the coals until they're red?
Keep the fire hot, brand the horse,
Ride it out until it's dead?

Dandelion blows on the wind,
Pavement dominates the seed.
With wind and water,
Cracks the concrete,
Demonstrates the power of the weed.

(Chorus)
You can divide the world in two:
The gardeners and the pruners.
One prepares the soil for you --
The other holds the shears.

(Chorus repeats)

<3 vs. $

credit Noah Howard, Matt Bostick, and Doris Staley for lyrics

It's the thing
that rules the world.
To some people,
it's everything.
For some people,
it's banana bread:
Fills your belly,
keeps you fed.

(chorus)
But money's not love,
Love isn't cheap.
Money is shallow:
Love runs deep.

It's a worrisome thing
in and of itself.
It's just a representation
of something else.

(chorus repeats)

Everybody here for the ride:
For love or money,
it's time to decide.
We seek time together
to share our love.
Leave for work,
push it aside:
lunch is spent staring
at pictures on desks.
Hours for dollars,
dollars are fine,
but no matter the paycheck,

you can't buy time.
Minutes to hours,
day to weeks,
pennies to dollars
to savings in banks --
with time and money,
quantify their worth
can't contain
this invisible truth:
Measure into a bucket
fill according to need,
Empty into the river:
send love downstream.

Teresa Staley

A native of Greensboro, NC, Teresa began writing poetry at age 12. She graduated from St. Andrews Presbyterian College in Laurinburg with a B.A. in English and Secondary Education and received the M.F.A. in Creative Writing from The University of North Carolina at Greensboro, where she studied with Fred Chappell, Robert Watson and Lee Zacharias. She is a singer-songwriter with two CDs to her credit: Marijuana Wolf Gets Paid (2007) and Yank Your Blue Jeans Matching Parkas (2013). Her poems have been published in The Greensboro Review and Blue Pitcher.

Made in the USA
Lexington, KY
19 October 2017